ANIMAL TAILS

Retold by Geraldine McCaughrean

Series Advisor Professor Kimberley Reynolds

Illustrated by Alex Wilson and David Pavón

OXFORD
UNIVERSITY PRESS

Letter from the Author

Animals share our lives from the start. Cuddly beasts and cartoon animals are often our first and favourite friends. Our early stories swarm with animals – gentle at first, then more wolfish, but still less scary for the villains being furry.

For centuries, storytellers have depicted animals – but mostly animals behaving like humans. Eight hundred years ago, *Roman de Renart* told of mischievous (but likeable) Reynard the Fox. Two thousand years beforehand, Aesop was writing his fables. Age-old myths in Africa are almost always about animals ... Except that they are not, of course. Deep down, they are all about us. The naughty monkey, noble horse, proud lion, deadly tiger, clever rabbit, wise owl and faithful dog all represent the different kinds of people who live in the world, and their stories teach us how to deal with them.

Ask yourself: which kind of animal are you? Wise owl, shy mouse, lurking crocodile or king of the jungle?

Geraldine McCaughrean

Reynard
and Chanticleer

The farmhouse was nothing much –
one room above another, with a leaky
roof on top. But the woman who lived there
had two good strong daughters who helped
her run the farm. They worked hard and they
slept well. In the yard were three cows, a
sheep, a goat, a pond and a clutch of chickens.

Oh, and there was an old cockerel, too.

Now open wide your ears and hear the
splendorous history of this noble cockerel!
Crowned at birth with the name of Chanticleer,
no cockerel in all the land could crow more
gloriously. His forehead blazed with a scarlet
crest. His coppery beak gleamed, and his
legs and feet were of such blueness that they
outshone both sky and sea. Around his

shoulders hung a cloak of golden plumes. This king – this emperor of cockerels – had seven lovely wives, each robed in gorgeous gowns trimmed with gold. But the fairest wife by far was Madam Pertelote.

Their love for one another was renowned throughout the realm.

One early morning, Chanticleer woke Pertelote with cries of, 'O woe! O woeful woe! Such a terrible dream!' (His wife opened a glittering eye.) 'I was walking in the grounds of this, our palace, beside the ornamental lake when, all of a sudden, out leaped a ferocious beast. Its coat was red, its nose as sharp as any sword, its ears tipped with black – and its tail was a fiery jet of flame! Oh, those teeth! Those blazing eyes!'

'Bck bck bck, it's just a dream,' cried his fair beloved. 'You know your trouble: you ate too much last night.'

'Oh, but bird of birds! Hen of my heart! Dreams are often sent from heaven as warnings to great men! My dream was a warning!'

Madam Pertelote pecked him in the neck. 'Prunes. That's what you need,' she said.

Chanticleer opened his wings, like the banners of a knight riding into battle.

Unfortunately, the perch was narrow and he fell off. So since the sun was up, he went outside and began to crow.

Chanticleer stretched his noble neck and crowed with all his might. There was a butterfly fluttering about the palace grounds. Chanticleer began composing a poem about Spring and Life and suchlike, as he watched the butterfly flutter by and settle on a spray of leafy loveliness.

And there, crouching in the selfsame bush, was the very beast of his nightmare, jaws wide, teeth as curved and sharp as scimitars.

'Oh Death, I see thy horrid shape!' cried Chanticleer, and made to fly off.

'Do not distress yourself, majestic bird,' said the beast. 'For I am the Knight of the Burning Firebrand, and I have travelled many a mile to gaze upon the legendary Chanticleer. I see now that the rumours were all true of your splendour. And you sing as beautifully as any nightingale! Sing, oh do, marvellous bird, that I may drink in the sound!'

Chanticleer could not, in all chivalry, refuse such a flattering request. He stretched his neck towards the brassy disc of the rising sun and sang:

'COCK-A-DOODLE-SPLERGCK – UK-UK.' Glancing out of her door, the farmer saw her old cockerel standing by the duck pond staring at the mint patch when, suddenly, out jumped a bony red fox, grabbed the cockerel by the neck and ran off. The farmer dropped everything and snatched up a broom.

Oh woe and thrice woe! What grieving was in the halls of the King when the news reached Chanticleer's wives that their lord and master had been seized by the Knight of the Burning Firebrand!

'Paint the sun black and let there never be another worm eaten! Oh woe and double woe!' said the hens.

Swinging her broom, the farmer called her
two daughters, the man from next door and
Colly the dog, and they all splashed through
the farmyard puddles to chase the thieving fox.

'Drop it, you mangy pest, or I'll knock your
ears off!'

Chanticeleer, banging up and down on the fox's back, was as good as dead. But with his last breath, he managed to splutter, 'You've got 'em licked, you cunning old beast. They wouldn't catch you now if they ran all morning. You should see the looks on their faces. All as red as beetroots – you should see.'

Reynard the Fox could not resist. He turned in his tracks and stuck out his tongue. 'Na-na-n'na-naa-–Wha–?'

The cockerel fell out of his mouth and fluttered up into a tree.

'Oh, dash it all,' said Reynard.

Listen and listen well to the sermon Chanticleer preached from his high and leafy pulpit that day.

'Shame on you, ignoble fox, and on your whole foxy tribe for this outrage against the royal person of Chanticleer! The fox has been outfoxed. Never again will your sharp

fangs tear my feathery cloak! And may you
learn by today and mend
your bandit ways!'

'Ah, go on,'
said Reynard.
'Jump down and give
us another song. You
know you want to.'

'You're joking!'
spluttered Chanticleer.
'What kind of a dumb
cluck do you take
me for?'

All Aboard

Cats don't like water. So you'd think they would have been first aboard. When the world was swallowed up by water, and there stood this huge wooden ship, gangplank down and Noah beckoning the animals aboard, you'd expect the cats to be already curled up in the warmest corner of the ark.

But no. Because when the flood came, there were no cats. It happened in the Pre-Cat Age. Hard to imagine, but there you are.

Noah did not pick or choose his passengers. He had been told to take two of everything.

You and I might have left behind the scorpions, millipedes, tarantulas and asps, but Noah invited two of everybody ...

Except rats.

Rats nibble and gnaw. They gnaw and nibble. They also breed. Between the first flash of lightning and bang of thunder, two rats squeezed under the door, uninvited. Before the treetops were underwater, two dozen rats were scampering and scuttling, nibbling and gnawing and breeding. They ate the food meant for other animals. They left their droppings in everyone's bed. But worst of all, they gnawed and nibbled the ark itself.

'What can I do?' Noah asked the lion. Lion sneezed once and sneezed again. Perhaps it was chaff from the horses' hay tickling his nose, or pollen from the bees, dust from the donkeys. Or perhaps it was lion magic.

From out of his nose fell two balls of fluff. The fluff turned over in mid-air and landed on four sprung paws: the world's first cats. They sprang from den to pen, from hump to rump, from table to stable, from shoulder to shelf. They hunted down the rats, and either ate them or chased them over the side. (Rats swim rather well.) The noise of scratching and scrabbling fell silent. The cats had bounced and pounced every rat out of the ark.

Except one.

One had gnawed its way right into the wall of the ark, chewing out a hole to hide in. It was meant as a hidey hole, but rats nibble and gnaw; they gnaw and nibble; they cannot help themselves. The rat in the wall kept on gnawing.

While the floodwater still lay deep over the mountain peaks, and the ark gently spun in the wind, Rat gnawed right through to wet.

The water outside came inside. Rat abandoned ship. The ark was leaking! Very soon now, Noah, his animals, his wife and children would sink back down to the washy wastes of an underwater world. Up came the water: up to Noah's knees, up to the eagles' beaks, up to the ostriches' ears. Up came the water ...

And up hopped Frog, *'Ribbet ribbet,'* to land in Noah's hand. Frog took one great breath which blew her up into a ball and, seeing her idea, Noah bunged her into the hole. Still droplets trickled in. Frog spread her four tiny feet, stretched them so wide that not one drop more could creep by her ... and the ark was saved.

'*Amphibious!*' cried the other animals in admiration. 'Frog is absolutely and totally *amphibious*!'

And so she was. For before the flood, she had lived in bushes and trees, afraid of water, terrified of drowning. Now she held her breath and held her breath, day after day, though she was seasick, sweating with fear, and her bulging eyes gazed out on dead cities, on shark and squid and a million drowned things.

When at last the ark ran aground, when the doors were opened, the sunlight let in and the animals let out, Noah gently prised Frog out of the hole in the hull and away she hopped. The cats thought about pouncing ... but seeing her strange new greenness, her icky-sticky skin, went back to hunting mice.

Noah would like to have rewarded her, but Frog had reward enough. All her tadpoles grew up green, with sticky-icky skin and feet as wide as paddles, as happy in water as they were happy on land. Their proud parents thought them absolutely and completely *amphibious*.

Good-Luck-Bad-Luck
and No-Good

Wa Tung loved horses. He dreamed horses. He saw horse tails in the clouds and white manes in the waves. But his mother said horses were not for boys, especially not poor boys who had work to do in the garden. Still, Wa Tung loved horses.

He rode the branches of trees to imaginary adventures. He drew horses in the earth with his fingertip. He even tied his handkerchief in knots: two corners for the ears and four bunchy legs.

'I wish you were real,' said Wa Tung, and gave his cloth horse a kiss.

A stranger passing by on the road gave him the strangest look, clicked the fingers of both hands, and turned round three times. Wa Tung watched him all the way down the road, spellbound, only turning round when

something snorted in his ear.

There stood a horse, with high-stepping hooves, a mane as red as copper, and ears as pointy as spearheads. Wa Tung mounted up in a moment.

But his mother came running out of the house, flicking a cloth and shouting at the big horse.

Unluckily, the horse could not see her. In making his pretend horse, Wa Tung had not wanted to cut holes in his only handkerchief, and so the handkerchief horse had no eyes (which, you will agree, is hard luck if you're a horse). Startled by the commotion, it stepped off the path and trotted directly across the garden beds. On it blundered – over the cabbages, over the marrows, over the flowers and berry bushes.

Wa Tung's mother wailed and shrieked

(which only made things worse). 'What bad luck have you brought me now, Wa Tung? Bad horse! Shoo! Bad horse! Wicked, Bad-luck horse!'

Wa Tung slid to the ground, and finally managed to grab Bad-Luck Horse by the nose, gently pushing him backwards the way he had come.

'What are you doing, foolish child?' protested his mother. 'Do you want to finish the job of wrecking my garden?'

But as Bad-Luck Horse stepped backwards into his own hoof prints, the trampled plants sprang up again, as strong as ever.

The marrow-skins healed; the berries flew back to their thorns; the flowers stood to attention like well-drilled soldiers.

'You see, Ma?' said Wa Tung. 'He's not a bad-luck horse, after all!'

Grudgingly, his mother agreed to rename the horse Bad-Luck-Good-Luck, and let him stay on. After all, she could see how much Wa Tung loved that horse.

The boy groomed Bad-Luck-Good-Luck every day, fed him and cleaned up behind him. But home was a tiny house, with one small room, and blind Bad-Luck-Good-Luck did not make a good lodger. Lamps were knocked over, the mats were torn, the milk was spilled and (owing to an honest mistake about baskets) the washing got badly chewed.

Finally, Wa 'Tung's mother banished Bad-Luck-Good-Luck from the house – from the county – from the whole province: even from the realm of Cathay itself.

Away galloped Bad-Luck-Good-Luck Horse, into a new corner of the atlas, and there he met a mare. That is to say, he heard her being chased with hobbles and lassoes, halters and whips. She was a wild one, that mare. Born with a temper so hot that no one could touch her, she had never been tamed. She had never carried a rider, pulled a chariot or left a horse fair without biting at least twelve people. They called her 'No-Good', and Bad-Luck-Good-Luck thought he had never smelled anyone so *marvellous*.

Though he missed Wa Tung most dreadfully, he thought it best if he and his wife stayed away from gardens and cottages and horse-breakers with whips. So they lived

in the seams of the world, in its
hidden valleys and river gorges,
until, one day, news
flowed downstream,
and they drank it at
the river bank:
War is coming.
The news set
the countryside
rumbling: *War is coming*.
Two great armies were
mustering, one on either side of
the Great Wall.

The Emperor had decreed
that all the young men
with horses must go and
fight. Wa Tung wanted
to do his duty like the
other young men in the
province, but he was too
poor to buy a horse.

'Good,' said his mother.

'I wish I still had Bad-Luck-Good-Luck,' said Wa Tung, 'or the money to buy a horse.'

'May you never grow rich, then,' said his mother. For the first time in her life, she was glad to be poor, because she did not want her son to go to the war.

Then something snorted into each of her ears, and when she turned round, there were two horses, one coppery red, one white, standing on the cabbages.

Bad-Luck-Good-Luck offered to carry Wa Tung to the war and No-Good Mare offered

to carry his pack. The boy's mother called him a bad-luck-bad-luck-worst-of-bad-luck horse, but seeing that her son was set on going, she relented and took hold of Bad-Luck-Good-Luck's nose. 'Bring him *good* luck – only *good* luck, you hear?' she begged, and kissed the horse on his no-eyes.

The armies stretched from East to West, twelve leagues from the Great Wall in one direction, twelve leagues from the Great Wall in the other. No-Good described what she could see. 'The banners carry the names of every warlord. The chain mail glints. The horses' hooves are oiled and shining, and their saddlecloths are ... '

'I know,' said Bad-Luck-Good-Luck. 'Since Wa Tung's mother kissed me, I can see clearly.'

'You can?'

'In my mind's eye. As the poet says, "My mind is a horse that flies like the wind. It gallops in the plains of great bliss".'

'Bliss? *Bliss?* They will all be slaughtered! So many sons will die! So many children will be left fatherless! So many wives will be widowed! So many mothers will be heartbroken!'

'No,' said Bad-Luck-Good-Luck.

'No?'

Bad-Luck-Good-Luck trotted to the top of a high hill and whinnied sharply. His voice, when he spoke, was as loud as thunder. 'FRIENDS! Brothers! Cousins! Comrades!'

A forest of ears swivelled.

'Horses suffer most in battle. The land suffers; the sweet grass is ploughed up and poisoned by tears. Colts die before their parents, which Nature never meant to happen! We know horses are more powerful than man. Oh, we let them think they are our masters, but we horses are free, because our minds are free!'

Then No-Good Mare spoke up, too. 'The first horse in the world was created when Sky sank spurs of lightning into the Earth. Our father Sky and our mother Earth do not want this war!'

'So let us end it before it begins!' shrieked Bad-Luck-Good-Luck. 'The Emperor and Generals say there will be a battle today. I say NAY!'

The answer came back:

'NEIGH! NEIGH! *NEIGH!*'

The sound of horses neighing rang out so loud that the mortar in the Great Wall shivered and trickled down like sand. Thirty thousand horses galloped into battle, darting and dodging each other. Their riders (who had no idea what was happening) strained to control their horses and swing their swords, but every stroke missed its mark.

A whirling wheel of horses swept together, swirling like a whirlpool, until the armies were hopelessly muddled. Then the wheeling horses pressed closer and closer together. Knee jolted against knee, thigh against thigh, shoulder against shoulder. There was no room to swing a sword: enemies were pressed together so tightly that their helmets clashed. They saw into each other's eyes. They smelled each other's sweat. They dropped their swords for fear of hurting themselves or their own comrades. Helmets fell off, and hair tumbled loose.

'NEIGH! NEIGH! NEIGH!' came
the cry.

Then every horse bolted in every direction,
carrying its rider as far as the mountains or
sea or hills or forest: away from war. The war
never happened, because the horses had said
'Neigh'.

Wa Tung's mother was tending her garden
when Wa Tung rode up the road. She dropped
her trowel, and ran to meet them. Her son
started to explain what had happened, but she
had already heard the news. Breathless from
running, she flung her arms around stallion
and mare. 'History will remember your names,
dear friends.'

'What, 'Good-Luck-Bad-Luck'?'
said Wa Tung.

'Never! Legend will call him
'Lucky Horse', and so do I.

History will call his mate 'Lucky's Wife', and so do I. Now come in, both of you, and have some oats ... '

Reynard and the Highway Robbery

By the look of it, someone's been fishing. Reynard would like some of that fish.

Hurrying ahead, he lies down in the road: a dead fox, if ever you saw one.

The fisherman throws Reynard in the cart:
his wife has always wanted a fox-fur collar.

A deeply happy fox, if ever you saw one.

Time to leave, but not without something
for the fox cubs back home.

The Ugly Duckling

Based on the story by Hans Christian Andersen

At last! *Tap-tap crackle-crackle peep-peep!* One by one, Mrs Duck's eggs broke open, and out struggled her little chicks. Golden and fluffy and adorable, they peeped their way, like a little yellow traffic jam, towards the river bank.

But Mrs Duck glanced back and saw that one egg was left unhatched – an egg much bigger than the rest. 'Wait a moment, children,' she said.

Her neighbour took a look. 'That's not a duck egg. Wrong colour. That there's a turkey egg,' she said.

What to do? Leave it to get cold? Or sit on it a little longer, just to be sure?

Next day, the big egg crackled, and two great, black feet stuck out.

'It does have very big feet,' Mrs Duck said to her neighbour.

'Told you. Turkey. I said, didn't I? Didn't I say? Nothing to do with you.'

But Mrs Duck had stood and sat guard over the egg for so long that she felt a kind of fondness for the hulking, scruffy object that spilled out of it.

'Put that in the river and it'll drown like a brick,' said her neighbour. 'That's a turkey, is that.'

But it did not sink.
The ugly duckling –
oh, and it had a face
only its mother could
love – took to
swimming
like …
well, like a
duck to water.
Dipping his
head below the water,
he tasted green weed
and it tasted almost
like happiness.
In fact, he swam
even better
than the other little
ducklings.

Oh, those pretty,
fluffy, delightful,
spiteful little ducklings!

'Ugly – blurch.'

'Why are you so ugly?'

'Too big!'

'Big feet! Big feet!'

His brothers and sisters peeped and pecked at the ugly duckling – tried to drive him away for fear their friends laughed at them for having such a lumpy, dumpy, frumpy brother.

'It looks like a tennis ball that has been chewed by a large dog,' declared the Grand Duckchess, looking down her nose. '*Must* we look at that ugly face every day? It spoils the view.'

And all of this the ugly duckling heard. Every birdy word. Pushed and pecked and poked, he learned to keep away from the other ducks. In fact, he moved farther and farther away, till he found himself walking, waddling, stumbling, wading and swimming away and away towards the sunset.

The sun, too, moved away for the winter, and the fields and marshes, the lanes and winds grew colder. Ugly Duckling hid himself away on the saltmarshes where the reeds rattled like feather quills, and the water lay ankle deep. Falling asleep one night, he did not see the ice creeping closer over the water, and he woke to find he could not move.

A farmer came by and saw him, kicked the ice and broke it like eggshell, hatching Ugly Duckling a second time. The kind farmer took him home to a warm house, where the children flung wide their arms in welcome.

It was a *terrifying* sight –
like scarecrows blowing in a gale
– gigantic creatures who ran towards him.

Ugly Duckling ran, too, in a panic – round
and around the little cottage, knocking over
bowls and stools and toddlers and buckets
… The farmer's wife shrieked, the children
laughed, the door opened and a boot kicked
Ugly Duckling out into wintertime.

Feather snow was falling. In fact, Ugly
Duckling looked up to see what bird had
shed its feathers, and saw six swans flying
overhead. The sight was so beautiful that it
pierced his heart like a fishhook and drew
it up into the sky. For a moment, just
for a moment.

He had never seen such birds before, and though they passed over in silence, he heard a kind of singing, more beautiful than any lark.

At last, a lark sang! Ugly Duckling woke. Somehow he had waddled his weary way through winter and into warmer weather.

He would stay among the reeds, even so. He had learned: there was nothing waiting for him out in the wide world but kicks and unkindness. He was just too ugly to be seen by eyes, so he resolved to stay hidden from any- and everyone.

Still, the river called to him. His big black feet longed to push a path through flowing water, to feel the current under him like the rush of his own bloodstream! He must swim in the river one last time!

Uh-oh.

There on the river was a family of swans. Where to go? Where to hide himself? Beauty cannot bear ugliness. So, obviously, these lovely, regal creatures would hate and detest him. Ugly Duckling upended himself, plunging his head deep underwater. When he could hold his breath no longer, he resurfaced ... and found himself under attack! The swans were rushing towards him, necks outstretched, black beaks ready to slice him in pieces!

Well, let them. Ugly Duckling stretched his head up high: at least he would die bravely!

'Little brother! Princeling! Friend!
Where is your flock? Where is your skein?
Where have you been hiding yourself?'
And their necks rubbed his, flexing, stroking, caressing him. The swans did not hate him!

From the river bank came the sound of the farmer's children.

Uh-oh!

They began to throw things.

Cake crumbs and bread crusts and words.

'A new one, look!'

'Oh, he's the best one, look.'

'Yes! Isn't he just the most beautiful swan who ever swam!'

Ugly Duckling bent his head and looked down at the sunlit water. His reflection looked back at him – a majestic swan, white as the clouds above, and plumed with happiness.

In fact, that swan was more wonderfully happy than any duck has been, in the whole quacking history of the rolling river.

A Tiger Tale

A wise Brahman was walking through the jungle when he heard the sound of mewling and misery coming from a hole in the ground. Looking into the matter, he saw a tiger of terrifying orange-stripyness, hurling itself at the sides of the pit and falling back amid a scatter of pebbles and earth.

Seeing the Brahman, the tiger called out, 'Oh help me, wise master! The people in the village dug a pit to trap me. My thirst is terrible! My suffering is fearful! A tiger must have freedom to roam the world!'

'Why would the people dig a pit to trap you?' asked the not-so-stupid Brahman. 'Were you perhaps killing and eating them?'

'Of course! That's what tigers do. It's in our nature.'

'Sadly, it is in the nature of humans not to like being killed and eaten by tigers.'

But Tiger wept and groaned and whimpered as if his heart would break from sorrow long before he died of hunger. 'If I die here in this pit, what will become of my poor wife and my fatherless cubs? Help me, won't you? Free me, and I will be a good vegetarian tiger for the rest of my days. Promise!'

The wise-but-sentimental Brahman was tempted to be kind. It is in the nature of Brahmans to be kind. He pitied poor Tiger.

'If you promise not to eat me …'

'Oh, I would never do that, holy master! If you help me, I will be like your pet dog, and serve you faithfully all my life!'

So the wise-but-really-quite-gullible Brahman looked around and found a long branch fallen from a tree, and dropped one end into the pit, so that Tiger could run up it into the happiness of freedom and sunlight.

Which he did, faster than you can ask, *Was* that wise?

'Holes make me hungry,' said Tiger, snagging the Brahman with his huge claws. 'Would you like me to eat you from the feet upwards, or the head downwards?'

'But you promised!' said the sadder-but-wiser Brahman. 'You gave your word!'

Tiger shrugged. 'Of course! That's what Tigers do. It's the law of Nature!'

'Ah, if you are talking law,' said the Brahman, in a rush, 'I would like a second opinion. Give me an hour to discover whether it is fair and legal for a tiger to eat the Brahman who saved his life.'

Tiger (who always liked to play with his food before eating it) smiled smugly and agreed. 'I will come with you, just in case you decide to run off.'

So the wise-and-hopeful Brahman told a nearby tree what had happened, and asked if Tiger was being fair.

'The world is a thankless place,' replied Tree, spreading its branches in a gesture of despair. 'I give shade and shelter to everyone who passes along this road. In return, they rip off my branches to feed their cows. One day they will cut me down for firewood. Stop complaining. Accept your fate.'

Tiger smiled more broadly and licked
his lips.

So the wise-but-discouraged Brahman told his story to a donkey on a treadmill, drawing water up from a well, and asked if Tiger was being fair. Donkey shrugged. 'Fair? Since when is life fair? While I've been breaking my back turning this wheel, my owners fed me. But I'm getting old; I am no use to them anymore. Next week they mean to kill me and make glue out of my hooves. Fate's unkind, but you can't buck it.'

Tiger gave Brahman a jolly push, and he fell to the ground with the tiger on top of him.

Quickly, the wise-but-desperate Brahman asked the road itself, 'Road, is it fair that I rescued this tiger and now he means to eat me?'

'Hair can be fair; life is invariably dark,' said Road philosophically. 'Here I lie, helping humans get from one place to another, and how do they thank me? They walk over my back in gritty shoes and drop their litter on me.'

Tiger smiled more broadly still, and sharpened his claws, like carving knives.

The wiser-but-desolate Brahman noticed a jackal by the roadside, watching and grinning. (Jackals always grin; they cannot help it; it's the way they are made.) 'Tell me, honoured Jackal, is it just and fair that this tiger, who I rescued from a pit, plans to eat me?'

Jackal drooped one ear and turned her head on one side. 'What? Say that again. I can't do long sentences.'

Again the wise-but-slightly-flatter Brahman explained about Tiger's promise, and about freeing Tiger, and Tiger breaking his promise. Again Jackal shook her head. 'Say it again slower. Don't understand.'

Irritated, Tiger himself explained, but with no more success.

'Could you write it down, maybe?' said Jackal.

'I don't have any paper,' said Tiger.

'And I can't read,' said Jackal. 'Can't take in talking-type words either. You'll just have to show me.'

Impatiently, Tiger picked up the Brahman by the scruff of his neck and lolloped back to the pit, Jackal trotting along behind.

'Behold: one pit,' said Tiger testily. 'Tiger in pit.'

'No you're not,' said Jackal. 'How did you get into the pit, anyway?'

'Well, I was *flung* in there, wasn't I?' blared Tiger, and flung himself dramatically into the pit. 'Along comes stupid Brahman. Stupid Brahman puts branch in pit. Tiger gets out. Tiger eats Brahman. Right?'

'Go back to the beginning, will you,' said Jackal scratching her head. 'Was the branch in the pit with the tiger at the start of the story?'

'Of course not, you dimwit! Or I could have got out, couldn't I?'

So Jackal pulled the branch out of the pit. 'Like that, you mean?'

'*Exactly*,' said Tiger.

Jackal pricked both ears. Her eyes gleamed, and she laughed her hacking little laugh.

'If you want my opinion, things are fair as they are.' And after dusting down the wise-but-delighted Brahman with her bristly tail, she trotted away, leaving the tiger raging and roaring in the bottom of the pit.

The wise-and-hilariously-happy Brahman went on his way down the road. But he did stop off at the treadmill by the well. He invited Donkey to join him on his travels, and she agreed, with delight.

'Got anything to eat?' enquired Donkey after a while.

'No. Brahmans own nothing but their life and their freedom and whatever wisdom they learn on the road. You may share that if you like?'

'I like,' said Donkey.

Let Me Go

Lions are a lazy lot. They spend long hours sleeping in the sun. They even send their wives out to do the hunting for them. So it was an easy mistake to make. Little Mouse thought it was safe to creep past the giant paws, the long, damp nose, the closed eyes, the wiry whiskers. But Big Lion was not asleep.

Gotcha!

One paw came down – *thud* – on poor Little Mouse, and knocked her flat. The other paw scooped her towards an open mouth.

'Wait! Wait! Please! Don't eat me! I am too small to do you good. At home I have twenty-two mouslings! You are King of Beasts and royalty shouldn't sink to cruelty!'

'I am a cat,' said Big Lion. 'Cats eat mice.'
And he rolled Little Mouse between the black,
scratchy pads of both front paws.

'Oh, but such a cat! Greatest of all cats! They call you King of the Jungle, and kings should be wise, gracious, merciful and large of spirit! I confess that I am the smallest and least important creature in your kingdom, but let me live, and one day I may do you some great service!'

Big Lion gave a throaty laugh that smelled of raw meat. 'What could you ever do for me, absurd rodent? Mice are too small to be useful.'

Just then, he caught sight of his wife dragging a dead gazelle home from hunting. He would eat well, no matter what, and he had rather liked those words: 'gracious', 'merciful' and 'large of spirit'. So he let Little Mouse go, and watched her speed over the ground as fast as the shadow of a wren. Before she was even out of sight, she was forgotten.

But Little Mouse did not forget.

Hunters more fearful than lionesses were hunting the plains of the Oko Vanga: poachers!

One sweltering noon, Lion lay down in the shade of a tree. Something dropped out of the branches overhead – something without a smell or even a shape. It smothered Lion in lines and loops, and when he tried to escape, tangled itself even more tightly around him.

A poacher's net.

Soon Lion lay parcelled, helpless, bulgy and – do not speak it out loud – very scared indeed. Strength could not burst the net, cunning could not free him; his lionesses had fled. A noise escaped Lion rather like kittens mewing.

'I will free you, Your Majesty,' said a little voice.

'Oh, Little Mouse, nothing can save me now from the poachers' knives,' moaned Big Lion.

Little Mouse had tiny teeth. She began to nibble at the cords of the net. Such tiny teeth, such coarse and hairy rope, but Little Mouse nibbled and spat, nibbled and spat, until there was a hole the size of a paw, a hole the size of a nose.

The ground rumbled like hunger. The poachers were coming back. But still Little Mouse nibbled and spat, nibbled and spat, until there was a hole the size of a lion's head, a lion's mane. Out through the hole came the head and behind it came all the rest of the King of Beasts, in a flailing scramble to be free.

Both Lion and Mouse set off to run. They did not run in the same direction, of course: mice and lions do not make good neighbours. But sometimes little acts of kindness are remembered for a lifetime. For the rest of her tiny timorous life, Little Mouse never forgot Big Lion who had spared her life. For the rest of his fierce and furry life, Big Lion never forgot Little Mouse, or the day she had saved his life.

Uluksak and the Bear

In the frozen country where night is a season long, a woman gave birth to twin boys.

'Oh dear, oh dear,' said the neighbours. 'A shame, a shame,' they sighed, shaking their heads over the cradle.

They said it twice because there were two baby boys. It was the two-ness that made them sigh. 'Bad luck, twins.'

'Double the boy, double the trouble.'

'And so hairy! Hairy like seal pups. Ergh.'

Though they were as fine a pair of babies as ever laughed at the moon, their parents could not ignore the looks on their neighbours' faces. Even they began to look at their boys with superstitious eyes. They gave the twins only one name between the two: Nanook.

Their cradle began to look like nothing but a box of bad luck, waiting, waiting to be opened. So at last, one sunless day, they dragged the cradle out of doors, emptied it out, and left the boys on the snow. The igloos were abandoned, the tribe moved on, moved on as all the creatures of the North move on, restless, looking for food.

Out on the snow, under the shooting stars, the baby boys shivered and cried. But they did not die.

One crawled south, south, towards spring until under his knees grew mosses and soil and flowers. His hair was long and dark. With time, it grew longer and darker. And at last, when he pulled himself to his feet, he was a bear, a big black bear, on the tundra.

Meanwhile, his brother crawled off the soft snow and onto hard ice, onto the frozen fringes of the sea, onto the growling ice floes. His hair was long and pale. With time, it grew longer and paler. And when at last he pulled himself to his feet, he was a polar bear, white and sleek and dangerous. In his giant paw he clutched the one-and-only name: Nanook.

In the frozen country where night is a season long, a woman gave birth to a boy and gave him the name Uluksak. He grew up to be a hunter.

One spring, an early thaw smashed the frozen sea like a mirror. It was bad luck for Uluksak the hunter, for there he stood, stranded on a crag of ice, surrounded by the sea. He could not jump to the frozen shore, and the thaw would only carry him farther and farther out to sea on a melting mound of ice.

He crouched on his island of ice. He called and yelled and wept. He ate all the fish he had caught on his hunt and he chewed the skin of his clothes. Numbly, he wondered whether it was better to starve or to drown in the icy sea. Then the iceberg lurched, and Uluksak slid spread-eagled across the ice towards the lapping water. He sank his knife in the slippery ice and clung on ... as a huge, fierce head rose up out of the sea.

Uluksak was looking into the eyes of a polar bear – a ravenous eater of meat. Surely Death itself was about to climb aboard the iceberg and feast on the helpless hunter. Such teeth! Such claws! Such an immense shawl of fur ... Uluksak opened his mouth to scream, but the bear opened his wider.

'I fear you are in trouble, cousin,' it said. 'Permit me to help you.' It sank once more from sight and, when it returned, its mouth was crammed with fish. With ponderous ease, the polar bear pulled itself on to the iceberg, laid the fish at Uluksak's head, and shook itself dry. It lay along the length of him, soft white fur warming the hunter, keeping off the wind.

And Death swam farther off, like a whale.

'My name is Nanook,' said the bear. 'In this frozen country, where night is a season long, a woman gave birth to me and my brother. We were as helpless as any newborn babies are. But we were twins, you see. The neighbours looked at us and shook their heads. "A shame, a shame," they said. Our parents abandoned us. But Nature did not: it simply shaped and suited us better to the land where we lived. So you see, we are cousins, my Inuit friend!' And the polar bear covered Uluksak's hand with its paw.

The wind turned about. The iceberg began to float back the way it had come. It carried Uluksak back to the shore, to the steaming, springtime snows.

Nanook stood up and walked to the brink of the iceberg.

'No one will believe me!' Uluksak called after him. 'They will say the cold played

tricks on me, that I lay here all alone. Give me something so that my wife and children, at least, will thank you as I thank you – for ever!'

The polar bear seemed to take no notice, only licked itself with a rasping tongue. But as it licked, it gathered a mat of hair which it twisted into a cord. A white cord. A bit like the cord which binds newborn babies to their mothers; a bit like the cord which binds the moon to the earth. And Nanook gave it to his cousin the hunter.

I have it still. Would you like to see it?

We Inuits know: if ever we find ourselves looking into the eyes of a polar bear, we shall see ourselves looking back. Come what may, come what might (and it may be death for either one of us), we think back to Nanook the polar bear, and we greet him as our cousin.

The Robin's Song

A flicker of wings, a flash of red.

'Where are you going to this lovely morning, little Robin?' said the cat. 'You look so fine in your smart red waistcoat.'

'I am going to sing to the King and Queen,' said Robin.

The cat stretched herself and curled one paw. 'Before you go, let me show you my white fur collar. Come closer. You have never seen the like.'

Robin tilted his head to one side and then the other. 'I can see it well enough from here, thank you,' said Robin. 'You have had many a little birdie for breakfast, but you shan't have me.' And away he flew.

A flicker of wings, a flash of red.

'Where are you going this lovely day, in your smart red waistcoat?' said the hawk.

'I am going to sing to the King and Queen,' said Robin.

The hawk spread its wings, drying the dew from his back. 'Before you go, let me show you the magic feather I have in my breast. You may wear it to the palace, if you like.'

Robin tilted his head to one side and then the other. 'I have feathers enough of my own, thank you. You have skewered many a little birdie for lunch, with your great grim beak, but you shan't skewer me.' And away he flew.

A flicker of wings. A flash of red.

'Where are you going to this sunny afternoon, in your smart red waistcoat,' said Reynard the fox.

'I'm going to sing to the King and Queen,' said Robin.

The fox raised up his ginger tail like a big, red exclamation mark. 'Before you go, pluck a tuft of fur from the tip of my tail. It will make a fine present for the Queen.'

Robin tipped his head to one side and winked. 'My song is gift enough to the Queen. I have seen you crunch-munch on ducks and chickens. But you shan't crunch-munch on me.' And away he flew.

A flicker of wings. A flash of red.

'Where are
you going to this
windy afternoon?'
asked the little girl
sitting on the gate.
'I wish I had a red
waistcoat like yours.'

'I am going to sing
to the King and Queen,'
said Robin.

The little girl
beckoned with one
finger. 'I have some
crumbly crumbs
here in my
pocket. Come
and share.'

Robin tipped
his head to one side
and then the other.

'Thank you, but no thank you. You would put me in a cage and want me to sing for you, but I fly where I like, and I sing where I choose.' And away he flew.

A flicker of flags. A flash of sunlight on glass. A flash of red sunset reflected in glass. Robin landed on the windowsill of the palace, and sang with all his might.

The King and Queen were delighted.

'I never heard a song so sweetly sung!' said the King.

'How smart he looks in his little red waistcoat. How shall we reward Master Robin for his kindness, this glowing evening?'

Robin tipped his head to one side and then the other.

'If it please you,' he said, 'let me marry Jenny Wren who hops about your garden from morning till night.'

'That's me,' said Jenny Wren, landing on the sill beside him.

So Robin and Jenny were married. And because kings and queens like to make a fuss, it was a grand wedding, with breadcrumbs and worms and nuts and berries. Guests came from far and wide, and danced and feasted for a week and a day.

(But I don't think they ate the worms.)

Whistle and They'll Come To You

Many animals are hunters, none more so than Man. And of all the hunters in the wild wide wilderness of China, Lo-Wun was the most ruthless. Determined to kill more deer than any hunter in history, he whittled a whistle out of bamboo – one which could mimic the voice of any animal in the forest. He slipped this wonderful whistle into his quiver of arrows and went hunting.

When he came to a clearing, he sat down, laid an arrow to his bow, and blew his whistle. It made a sound as soft as wool and exactly like the bleat of a young fawn. A mother deer – all tenderness and large liquid eyes – trotted into the clearing, looking for the fawn. And Lo-Wun shot her in the chest.

'Of all the world's hunters, Man is the best, and of all the men in China, I am best of all.'

Unfortunately, the sound of the whistle had carried. A hungry lynx thrust its head into the clearing. 'Did I hear the bleat of a fawn?' it asked.

Lo Wun turned a little pale, but he put his pipe to his lips and blew. The pipe growled like a tiger. The lynx stared at him with startled ears, and leaped away through the trees.

Lo-Wun laughed. 'Of all the world's hunters, Man is the cleverest, and of all the men in China, I am the cleverest of all!'

With a crackle of twigs and orange, flaming fur, a tigress bounded into the clearing.

'Did I hear the growl of a lusty tiger?' said the tigress. But when she saw only Lo-Wun sitting on the ground, her tongue dripped, and her claws stretched, and her green eyes flickered.

Lo-Wun turned ashy pale, but again he put the whistle to his lips and blew. The pipe made a sound that shook leaves from the trees – the throaty grumble of a grizzly bear. The tigress turned in terror and bounded away.

Lo-Wun wiped his brow. 'Of all the world's hunters, Man is the most daring, and off all the men in Chi—'

A paw tapped him on the shoulder – a paw with claws as long as grappling hooks, a paw brown and furry and huge.

'I heard the growl of a fellow bear, but I found only you,' said the grizzly bear, and taking the whistle from Lo Wun's mouth, he picked his teeth with it.

'Of all the men in China, I am the most stupid,' said Lo-Wun ... from inside the bear.

A Winter's Tale

One chilly day, Wolf and Reynard meet up. The locals are catching fish the winter way – through holes in the ice.

'Fish? Too right, Wolfie,' says Fox. 'Hundreds of 'em! This magic bucket lures them in. Shall we give it a try?'

Wolf wants first go: can't wait to catch supper in a magic bucket! Reynard does not argue. He even ties the bucket onto Wolf's tail.

Wolf sits on the ice, tail down the hole, the bucket tied to it.

Up comes
moon, like a slice
of ice. Down
comes frost and
freezes the pond.
It takes a while for
Wolf to notice:

his tail is frozen in ...

Howling, tugging,
straining and pulling,
Wolf rages at the moon.
'Look what you did to
my tail!'

But you and the
moon know better who
was really to blame.